BOLD BRAVE FAITH

CWR

CONTENTS

INTRO

Alright guys? So here it is – a great book just for us lads. A lot of time (and fun!) has gone into this, narrowing down what to include from the Bible. The hardest part was choosing, as it's all so brilliant! We hope you get as much out of it as has gone into it. We've selected four main themes that appeal more to us boys; ranging from teamwork and mates, temptation and how to resist it, Joshua and his battles, to attitudes and how to make sure we're living with the right outlook.

Enjoy!

'I have come that they may have life, and have it to the full.' **John 10:10**

TEAMWORK
ONE FOR ALL ...

'Greater love has no one than this: to lay down one's life for one's friends. You are my friends if you do what I command. I no longer call you servants, because a servant does not know his master's business. Instead, I have called you friends, for everything that I learned from my Father I have made known to you. You did not choose me, but I chose you and appointed you so that you might go and bear fruit – fruit that will last – and so that whatever you ask in my name the Father will give you.' **JOHN 15:13–16**

Unless you become a hermit or full-time couch potato, **YOU CAN'T AVOID MEETING PEOPLE.** This first series of Bible readings will kick off some thoughts on the way God wants us to get on with others.

What is friendship all about? Take the Mafia model, for example. A heavy 'Godfather' type chewing his gum, muttering to a trembling, sweaty-palmed character, 'Hey Greaso, you're like a brother to me. Don't let me down. We wouldn't want you to have a terrible accident, would we?' Such friendships are based on fear. The friendship God wants us to offer is not based on fear but on love. We are not to bully others into doing what we want or manipulate them to get our own way.

TRUE FRIENDSHIP IS ABOUT GIVING, NOT GETTING.

The disciples were always arguing over which one of them was the most important person in the team. They squabbled to get the best positions on the team sheet. So Jesus made them think about the way He treated them and the way they treated each other.

Jesus was their best Mate. He didn't treat them like dogsbodies or lapdogs. He showed them respect. They didn't know at the time, but soon Jesus was to show them the ultimate in friendship by dying to save them.

Think about the people you are likely to meet today and ask God to help you be a genuine friend to them.

'Love' sometimes comes across as a bit of a girly word. Jesus didn't expect His tough, macho disciples to suddenly become feminine. He wanted them to obey Him – now there's a challenge. The more we obey God the more sensitive we become to the needs of others.

WORLD CHAMPIONS

'Jesus went up on a mountainside and called to him those he wanted, and they came to him. He appointed twelve that they might be with him and that he might send them out to preach and to have authority to drive out demons. These are the twelve he appointed: Simon (to whom he gave the name Peter); James son of Zebedee and his brother John (to them he gave the name Boanerges, which means 'sons of thunder'), Andrew, Philip, Bartholomew, Matthew, Thomas, James son of Alphaeus, Thaddaeus, Simon the Zealot and Judas Iscariot, who betrayed him.' **MARK 3:13–19**

It was team photo time. Jesus had picked His squad for the *ALL-TIME CHAMPIONSHIP* of the world.

What a load of rubbish! No one reckoned Jesus' squad would get anywhere in the world championships. Peter (nicknamed 'The Rock') had a reputation for scoring own goals. Strikers James and John (nicknamed 'Sons of Thunder'), were certain to be booked or sent off. Simon, who hated the Romans, wouldn't pass to Matthew because he once worked for them. James the Less was too small. Jude was a nobody. Thomas doubted they could win anything. Bartholomew was a joker. And Judas was known to accept bribes from the opposition.

But Jesus turned them into champions (apart from Judas, who transferred himself for a record fee – 30 pieces of silver). How? Jesus pulled together a team that He could train to be champions. He was prepared to spend time working with them. He wasn't the kind of manager to sit in a suit in the Directors' Box. He was out there as a player-manager – **GETTING STUCK IN, ENCOURAGING, HELPING, ATTACKING AND SHOWING THEM HOW TO WIN.** That's the kind of Friend Jesus is. Someone who is alongside you wherever you are.

>ENGAGE

What kind of friend are you? Someone who keeps their distance or someone who gets alongside other people? Jesus wants us to mix in and help others. This is never an easy thing to do, particularly if you are shy, but God can give you the confidence you need.

PRAY

Father, help me to be a good friend, even if it seems difficult. Amen.

MYSTERIOUS STRANGER

'Andrew, Simon Peter's brother, was one of the two who heard what John had said and who had followed Jesus. The first thing Andrew did was to find his brother Simon and tell him, "We have found the Messiah" (that is, the Christ). And he brought him to Jesus.

Jesus looked at him and said, "You are Simon son of John. You will be called Cephas" (which, when translated, is Peter).' **JOHN 1:40–42**

When Andrew was given the lowdown on a passer-by, he chased after Him. He wanted to get to know this stranger and find out more about Him. *WHO WAS ANDREW'S NEW FRIEND?*

Andrew had made a mind-blowing discovery. His new Friend was none other than the One that God had sent to save the world. Just think of the name-dropping he could do: 'I was only saying to the Saviour of the World the other day …' And the two of them had got on so well together. In fact, they had chatted for most of the day. Andrew discovered that Jesus was scouting for players to join His world championship squad, and was eager to play.

Would Andrew keep his meeting with Jesus quiet? After all, you don't want others **MUSCLING IN** on the team and threatening your place. No, Andrew was a good friend. He immediately brought his talented brother Simon Peter along for a trial. Jesus got on famously with Simon and He gave him a new nickname – 'Rocky'. Andrew was not jealous when Jesus hinted that Peter might become captain of His team. Nor did he get upset that Jesus had not given him a nickname. Andrew was just pleased to share his Friend with others.

>ENGAGE

Some people have a gang mentality to friendship. You are either accepted as one of a small group of friends or rejected. You are in or out. Some can be afraid of losing their status or feel threatened when new people come into their circle of friends. Jesus doesn't want us to shut others out of our friendships. He wants us to reach out to others. Chat to God first, then look for opportunities to introduce Jesus to other people.

PECKING ORDER

'He came to Simon Peter, who said to him, "Lord, are you going to wash my feet?"

Jesus replied, "You do not realise now what I am doing, but later you will understand."

"No," said Peter, "you shall never wash my feet."

Jesus answered, "Unless I wash you, you have no part with me."

"Then, Lord," Simon Peter replied, "not just my feet but my hands and my head as well!"' **JOHN 13:6–9**

▶ In most groups a **_CHAIN OF COMMAND_** can be seen – a natural leader or alpha male, some taggers-on, some who flit in and out between groups – everyone knows their place. But what happens when the pecking order is challenged?

Someone was needed to clean the boots and there wasn't an apprentice around to do it. In fact it was more than the boots; everyone needed their sweaty feet washed. Rocky (Simon Peter) didn't budge. As aspiring captain of the squad, he turned his nose up at the job.

To Rocky's embarrassment, Jesus, the team's highly respected Manager, grabbed a bowl of water and began to wash their smelly feet. Rocky couldn't handle this.

He didn't mind the others flushing the dirt out from between his toes, but he felt uneasy that Jesus should be doing it.

When Jesus pointed out that it was an **ACT OF FRIENDSHIP,** Rocky suddenly wanted Jesus to hose down his hands and scrub the back of his neck. There was nothing that Rocky wanted more than to be seen as a friend of Jesus.

>ENGAGE

Jesus built up good team morale by mucking in to help His friends. His actions gave great authority to His team-talk about caring for each other. How do you react when there are unpopular tasks to be done at home, school or church? Do you turn up your nose or roll up your sleeves? Talk to the team Manager now and ask Him to train you to be a good friend to those in need.

UNDER PRESSURE

'"A new command I give you: love one another. As I have loved you, so you must love one another. By this everyone will know that you are my disciples, if you love one another."

Simon Peter asked him, "Lord, where are you going?"

Jesus replied, "Where I am going, you cannot follow now, but you will follow later."

Peter asked, "Lord, why can't I follow you now? I will lay down my life for you."

Then Jesus answered, "Will you really lay down your life for me? Very truly I tell you, before the cock crows, you will disown me three times!"' **JOHN 13:34–38**

What makes a great team? Good managers work long and hard to build up good team spirit. But Jesus had a squad of squabblers and in-fighters. It would take a miracle to get them playing as a team.

Christians – how are they different? Jesus pointed out that those in His squad would be noted for their close friendship with each other. No matter who was in the team, they would be accepted, helped and involved. Everyone was important, each had a part to play, and **NO MAN WAS LEFT BEHIND.**

Rocky (Simon Peter) was emerging as captain of the world championship squad. But, although he was great when they were winning, when things started to go wrong he was liable to walk off the pitch. In the dressing room before the big match he told Jesus he would give everything, **EVEN IF IT KILLED HIM.** Jesus knew His players well. He warned Peter that the whistle would be blown on him three times and he would let the whole team down. Some example for a captain to give!

Rocky wanted to be a good friend to Jesus and his team-mates, but under pressure he was liable to ditch them. However, even though Jesus knew Rocky would let Him down, He didn't drop him or take away his captaincy.

>ENGAGE

Jesus is a great Friend even when we are disloyal. He knows that we need His help to love and accept others. Ask Him to teach you how to be a friend on whom others can rely.

PRAY

Father, help me to be there for my friends, to listen and not judge. Help me to be a friend like Jesus. Thank You for always being there for me. Amen.

DENIED

'Jesus stood on the shore, but the disciples did not realise that it was Jesus. He called out to them, "Friends, haven't you any fish?"

"No," they answered.

He said, "Throw your net on the right side of the boat and you will find some." When they did, they were unable to haul the net in because of the large number of fish.

Then the disciple whom Jesus loved said to Peter, "It is the Lord!" As soon as Simon Peter heard him say, "It is the Lord," he wrapped his outer garment round him ... and jumped into the water.' **JOHN 21:4–7**

▶ When team players have a bust-up with their managers, they are likely to be dropped from the team or transferred to another club. What would Jesus do with Rocky, the captain who had let the whole side down?

Rocky had been anything but a good team captain. When an angry mob invaded the pitch to get rid of the Manager, Rocky went shaky, swearing that he had never played for Jesus' team. He lied three times before racing off, leaving Jesus to be crucified.

DID JESUS HARBOUR A GRUDGE

against Rocky? No. When Jesus rose from the dead He looked Rocky up and they had a confidential chat. At the end they were great friends again. **JESUS WAS BACK IN CHARGE** and He wanted Rocky to be part of His new team – a team that would conquer the world for Jesus.

Later, on Peter's home pitch of Galilee, Jesus appeared on the sideline. Rocky was over the moon to see Jesus again and went overboard with delight. He didn't mind taking an early bath. Jesus showed there were no hard feelings between Him and Rocky by cooking him breakfast. It was the best fish and ships (sorry!) Peter had ever had.

>ENGAGE If our friends let us down we can feel extremely hurt. And the closer the friendship, the deeper the hurt can be. Jesus wants us to forgive those who betray our trust and do all we can to rebuild the friendship. Have you been upset by a friend recently? Don't keep your distance. Talk it through with God and ask Him to team you up again.

BACK IN THE TEAM

'Jesus said to Simon Peter, "Simon son of John, do you love me ...?"
"Yes, Lord," he said, "you know that I love you."
Jesus said, "Feed my lambs."
Again Jesus said, "Simon son of John, do you love me?"
He answered, "Yes, Lord ... I love you."
Jesus said, "Take care of my sheep."
The third time he said to him, "Simon son of John, do you love me?"
... He said, "Lord, you know all things; you know that I love you."
Jesus said, "Feed my sheep."'

JOHN 21:15–17

Rocky was back in the team and Jesus was planning to enlarge His squad. Who would be captain of this **DYNAMIC, POWERFUL, WORLD-BEATING** side? Rocky had surely blown his chances of leading.

Jesus took Rocky (Peter) aside to discuss His plans for the future. Three times Jesus asked Rocky if he really wanted Him to be his Boss. Rocky replied that he would play his heart out for Jesus. He loved his Boss and would give his all for Him.

Rocky knew that he had denied being part of the team three times, so it was no surprise that his commitment was questioned three times. Even so, he was as sick as a parrot each time Jesus raised the matter. Then came the good news. Jesus was **PUTTING HIM IN CHARGE** of the new team. He would be responsible for training the new recruits to Jesus' team, coaching them to live as Jesus wanted. Jesus then told Rocky he would be responsible for the rest of the squad too – training them to live God's way, showing them the tactics God had for defeating their opponents. Rocky would become player-manager, looking after the team's welfare on and off the pitch. Peter had expected to be relegated, not promoted. Here we go … here we go … here we go …

>ENGAGE

Jesus got alongside Peter and involved him in all He did. He was willing for Peter to share some of His responsibilities even when He knew Peter would make a hash of it. Are you prepared to involve others in the things you do?

PRAY

Lord, please open my eyes to the people around me. Help me to see whether there are people You want me to befriend. Amen.

GET INVOLVED

'Thomas said to him, "Lord, we don't know where you are going, so how can we know the way?"

Jesus answered, "I am the way and the truth and the life. No one comes to the Father except through me. If you really know me, you will know my Father as well. From now on, you do know him and have seen him."

Philip said, "Lord, show us the Father and that will be enough for us."

Jesus answered: "Don't you know me, Philip, even after I have been among you such a long time?"' **JOHN 14:5–9**

It's time to leave Rocky and see how other people fitted into Jesus' team. Philip was on the side when Jesus fed over 5,000 travelling supporters with five loaves and two fishes. Impressive stuff, but Philip still wasn't sure if Jesus really was God's Son.

Philip had seen Jesus perform many miracles but **STRUGGLED TO ACCEPT** who He really was. He could not work out how being a friend of Jesus made you a friend of God. How could getting to know Jesus be the same as getting to know God? Unless Jesus *was* God … 'Prove it,' said Philip. 'Let me see God and I'll believe.'

Philip shows that it is possible to work closely with someone for a long time without ever getting to know them or understanding what makes them tick. Despite hearing Jesus speak God's words and seeing Him use God's power, Philip kept a respectful distance. He was prepared to be a linesman on the sideline but not a player on the pitch.

Jesus pointed out that Philip needed to **GET INVOLVED** alongside Him and see God in action. He needed to tackle his doubts and go forward with Jesus.

>ENGAGE

How long have you been a Christian? How well have you got to know God in that time? God doesn't want you to be a spectator; He wants to encourage you to get involved, to talk to Him and to be part of His plan. Talk with a Christian you trust about the ways in which you can get to know and support each other. Kick off by praying for each other and your friends who do not know Jesus.

PRIDE AND PREJUDICE

'The next day Jesus decided to leave for Galilee. Finding Philip, he said to him, "Follow me."

Philip, like Andrew and Peter, was from the town of Bethsaida. Philip found Nathanael and told him, "We have found the one Moses wrote about in the Law, and about whom the prophets also wrote – Jesus of Nazareth, the son of Joseph."

"Nazareth! Can anything good come from there?" Nathanael asked.

"Come and see," said Philip.' **JOHN 1:43–46**

When a Soviet cosmonaut and an American astronaut shook hands in space for the first time, it was hailed as a great historical achievement. But when it was announced that it took place directly over Bognor Regis, on the English south coast, **NO ONE COULD TAKE IT SERIOUSLY.** Nathanael had a similar problem.

Nazareth was a town of tradesmen and poorly-educated peasants. It didn't have Premier League status. It was the last place the well-to-do wanted to live. Intellectuals and the aristocracy congregated in the better suburbs of Jerusalem and towns in the south.

Nathanael showed what a snob he was by looking down his nose at Jesus just because He came from Nazareth. Although Jesus knew of Nathanael's prejudices, He greeted him warmly and paid him a compliment. By **BUILDING UP THE PERSON WHO HAD PUT HIM DOWN,** Jesus got their first meeting off to a positive start.

Once Nathanael had got to know Jesus, he realised how foolish it was to make judgments about people based on where they live. By the end of their conversation, Nathanael held Jesus in very high esteem. He realised that Jesus was God's Son, the King of the Jews, and **WHAT AN HONOUR IT WOULD BE TO JOIN HIS TEAM.**

>ENGAGE

It's easy to make judgments about people because they live in a poor or rich neighbourhood. Do you shun or poke fun at those from different backgrounds to your own? It is only when we make the effort to get to know people that we realise how foolish it is to judge them by their appearance or where they live. Jesus invited rich and poor people to be in His team. Ask God to help you appreciate people for who they are rather than where they come from.

ENEMY TERRITORY

'As the time approached for him to be taken up to heaven, Jesus resolutely set out for Jerusalem. And he sent messengers on ahead, who went into a Samaritan village to get things ready for him; but the people there did not welcome him, because he was heading for Jerusalem. When the disciples James and John saw this, they asked, "Lord, do you want us to call fire down from heaven to destroy them?" But Jesus turned and rebuked them. Then he and his disciples went to another village.' **LUKE 9:51–56**

Jesus took His world championship squad into Samaria. The Samaritans were a difficult side and treated any encounters with Jews as *GRUDGE MATCHES.* Nothing friendly about this clash.

Two of the team were shown the red card before they reached the pitch and the match was abandoned. Some of Jesus' team were furious with the way the Samaritans treated them and *WANTED TO GET THEIR OWN BACK.* James and John, the temperamental strikers (remember the Sons of Thunder?), wanted God to incinerate the Samaritans by shooting a fireball from heaven.

Jesus knew about the long, bitter feud between the Jews and the Samaritans. However, He had not come to fuel the fighting but to quench it. **HE LOVED THE SAMARITANS AS MUCH AS HE DID THE JEWS.** It was part of His world championship plan that one day the Samaritans would accept Him as their Saviour and be part of His squad. It would be up to people like Rocky and the Sons of Thunder to befriend the Samaritans, tell them about Jesus and involve them in the team.

Jesus told James and John that they were way offside and warned them about their attitude. Years later, James and John were delighted to hear that many Samaritans had believed in Jesus and received the Holy Spirit. They welcomed them into the team.

PRAY

> *Lord Jesus, thank You that You love everyone, no matter where they come from or what other people think of them. Please help me to treat people like that too. Amen.*

SONS OF THUNDER

'Jesus called them together and said, "You know that those who are regarded as rulers of the Gentiles lord it over them, and their high officials exercise authority over them. Not so with you. Instead, whoever wants to become great among you must be your servant, and whoever wants to be first must be slave of all. For even the Son of Man did not come to be served, but to serve, and to give his life as a ransom for many."' **MARK 10:42–45**

Remember those twin strikers, James and John? They were nicknamed the **SONS OF THUNDER,** or should it have been the Sons of Blunder? Read on and decide for yourself.

James and John considered themselves to be more important than other members of the team. They went to Jesus demanding a better contract and seats on the Board.

Jesus warned them that ruling over others often involved pain, not gain. Before Jesus would rule in heaven He would need to suffer and die for others. 'Are you willing to do the same?' He asked them. James and John blundered along not understanding the deal Jesus was proposing. When the rest of the team heard what had been going on there were unpleasant rumblings about the Sons of Thunder. Jesus called a team meeting to clear the air. His message was plain and simple: 'If you want to be great in My team, you must **LEARN TO HELP OTHERS.** I am not in this world championship for what I can get, but for what I can give. And I am prepared to **GIVE MY LIFE** so that you can be in the winning team.'

>ENGAGE **Some people use friendships to advance their cause. They lick the boots of those above them and tread on those beneath them. Jesus wouldn't tolerate this attitude on His team. Teamwork was not about getting to the top of the pile but supporting and serving each other. It's what Jesus coached into His players and it was also the way He played. Talk with Jesus now and ask Him to train you as a good supporting player. It's the only way you'll become great in His team.**

RIVALRY

"'Our friend Lazarus has fallen asleep; but I am going there to wake him up."

His disciples replied, "Lord, if he sleeps, he will get better." Jesus had been speaking of his death, but his disciples thought he meant natural sleep.

So then he told them plainly, "Lazarus is dead, and for your sake I am glad I was not there, so that you may believe. But let us go to him."

Then Thomas (also known as Didymus) said to the rest of the disciples, "Let us also go, that we may die with him.'" **JOHN 11:11–16**

Jesus and His team had a difficult fixture in Bethany. Rival fans had attempted to throw stones at them during their last visit and some of the team *FEARED FOR THEIR SAFETY.*

Jesus knew He was heading for the most difficult away trip of His life. His season on earth was coming to an end and He needed to die and then live to *CLINCH VICTORY.* The members of Jesus' team did not expect such a dramatic finish. They knew that Bethany was near to Jerusalem and a violent mob was out to get Jesus. It seemed far easier to cancel the rest of their fixtures, drop out of the league and relax near Jordan.

Jesus wanted to get to Bethany to comfort His friends and bring Lazarus back to life. Difficult fixtures and opposition are part of God's plans. They are not to be avoided but faced in God's strength. Jesus headed off to face His next opponents. Thomas, who doubted the team could win anything, was moved by Jesus' willingness to go ahead. Although he feared they would all be killed, he told the rest of the team to stay together and support their Manager. **JESUS HAD NEVER LET THEM DOWN** and it was time for them to show their loyalty and support.

>ENGAGE

Are you the kind of friend who stays loyal in difficult times? Who do you know who needs help and support at this moment? What can you do to show them you are thinking of them and trying to understand what they are going through? Is there anything you can do to help them? Can you motivate others to get alongside them? Why not pray for them now.

PRAY

Father, help me to be around for my friends and encourage them through the things they are experiencing. Help me to know when to speak and when to listen. Amen.

OUTCASTS

'Then Levi held a great banquet for Jesus at his house, and a large crowd of tax collectors and others were eating with them. But the Pharisees and the teachers of the law who belonged to their sect complained to his disciples, "Why do you eat and drink with tax collectors and sinners?"

Jesus answered them, "It is not the healthy who need a doctor, but those who are ill. I have not come to call the righteous, but sinners to repentance."'

LUKE 5:29–32

Jesus faced a lot of criticism over His team selections. **WHY DID HE PICK THE BAD PLAYERS** that no one else wanted in their teams?

Tax collectors were outcasts because they worked for the Romans occupying the land. Most were thieving cheats, charging their fellow Jews more than was required and pocketing the difference. Matthew had a key post, taxing the traders moving their goods in and out of Capernaum. The fishermen in Jesus' team knew him well. He had overcharged every time they tried to market their fish out of town. No one wanted anything to do with Matthew – except Jesus.

Jesus invited Matthew to join His team. What was Jesus thinking? Matthew would be bad for team morale. Almost everyone else in the team had a **SCORE TO SETTLE** with him. There was more trouble when Jesus went scouting for recruits among Matthew's friends. Most were shady villains and underworld gangsters. The holier-than-thou Pharisees criticised Jesus for associating with such characters.

Jesus told them how He went about His team selection: 'I haven't come to headhunt those who think they are OK with God. I have come to invite those who want to change their ways and be made right with God to join My team.'

>ENGAGE Is there anyone you know who is snubbed or disliked by others, possibly because of some mistake they have made in the past? How would Jesus want you to treat that person? Talk the matter over with Him now and ask for His help in winning a new teammate.

VALUED YOUTH

TEAMWORK

'Some women were watching from a distance. Among them were Mary Magdalene, Mary the mother of James the younger and of Joseph, and Salome. In Galilee these women had followed him and cared for his needs. Many other women who had come up with him to Jerusalem were also there.' **MARK 15:40–41**

Are you the youngest member of your family or the smallest person in your class? It's never easy to be part of a team when everyone else is older or taller than you. Just ask young James.

There were two people called James in the team. So how would they tell them apart? One was the much-feared striker James (one of the Sons of Thunder). **NO ONE MESSED WITH HIM!** The other was a young lad whose parents came to watch him play. (Every time you read about him his mother or father also gets a mention.) The team called him James the Younger or James the Less.

Why did Jesus take such a risk with a young in-experienced person in His team? **JESUS VALUES WHAT YOUNG PEOPLE CAN OFFER** and wants them to strike out for Him.

Young James learnt from Jesus and was given a great opportunity to become a star. When Jesus was crucified, all the older, more experienced players ran off. Had James stayed he would now be known as James the Hero, but he bottled out of the challenge. His mother stayed to give Jesus support. If only young James had been as brave as she was.

>ENGAGE

Don't ever think you are too young to play an important part in God's plans. God wants to train you and bring you on in His team. Neither should you poke fun at anyone who is younger or smaller than you.

PRAY

God, thank You that I can play an important part in Your plans. Help me to take opportunities You give me to serve You. Amen.

REUNITED

'Then the apostles returned to Jerusalem from the hill called the Mount of Olives, a Sabbath day's walk from the city. When they arrived, they went upstairs to the room where they were staying. Those present were Peter, John, James and Andrew; Philip and Thomas, Bartholomew and Matthew; James son of Alphaeus and Simon the Zealot, and Judas son of James. They all joined together constantly in prayer, along with the women and Mary the mother of Jesus, and with his brothers.' **ACTS 1:12–14**

When Jesus died, His team disbanded. When *JESUS ROSE FROM THE DEAD,* He got them back together again. What would happen to them once Jesus left for heaven?

Meeting Jesus after He had risen from the dead was great for team morale. Even Thomas finally believed that with Jesus to help, nothing could stop them from winning. When Jesus left for heaven He promised He would send them a new Coach, the Holy Spirit, *TO ENCOURAGE THEM,* train them, build them up and show them winning tactics.

What would the team do while they waited for their new Coach to arrive? They regularly met together to talk to God. Notice that this team meeting was not just for the lads; the girls in Jesus' team were there too. They were the ones who hadn't run off to hide when Jesus was killed. Remember that next time you think of girls as weaker or less brave.

GOD HAS ALL KINDS OF PEOPLE IN HIS TEAM and it is important that they meet regularly to train together, plan their moves and talk to God.

>**ENGAGE**

Do you meet with other Christians to learn from the Bible and worship God? You can't expect to play your part in a team if you miss training and get unfit. Talk with the team members at your youth group (or other similar group you might be part of) about how you can work together to carry out God's plans.

PRAY

Lord, thank You for the Church. Thank You for people I can meet with, talk and pray with, and find out more about You with. Amen.

OFFSIDE RULE

'Mary took about half a litre of pure nard, an expensive perfume; she poured it on Jesus' feet and wiped his feet with her hair ... But one of his disciples, Judas Iscariot, who was later to betray him, objected, "Why wasn't this perfume sold and the money given to the poor? It was worth a year's wages." He did not say this because he cared about the poor but because he was a thief; as keeper of the money bag, he used to help himself to what was put into it.' **JOHN 12:3–6**

One member of Jesus' squad never made it into the world championship team. Judas arranged a transfer for **30 PIECES OF SILVER.** Why did he want to leave?

Judas was given the role of club treasurer. It was his job to manage the funds and give money to the poor. Jesus not only preached to the poor but also gave to them. Having access to this money was to play a part in Judas's downfall. **GREED TOOK OVER,** and he began to dream of what he could do with a little extra cash. Judas began stealing money from the club funds and putting it aside for his retirement. Jesus knew what was going on but He said nothing. When Judas saw

Mary pour expensive ointment on Jesus (worth a year's wages) he gasped at the waste of money! **HE DIDN'T REALLY CARE ABOUT THE POOR.** Just think how much he could have siphoned off if Mary had sold her bottle instead.

Judas found another way to get his money – he left the team and betrayed Jesus. It was Judas's decision to leave; Jesus never wanted to get rid of him. Sadly, soon afterwards, Judas committed suicide.

>ENGAGE

Even when we do things wrong, Jesus doesn't kick us out of His team. He knows what we get up to and gives us time to get onside. While we are being disobedient, a lot of our efforts are disallowed. We don't win our battles because we are constantly offside. Is God flagging for some offence He wants to bring to your attention? Sort it out with Him now and get back into the action.

THE MOTIVATOR

'When the day of Pentecost came, they were all together in one place. Suddenly a sound like the blowing of a violent wind came from heaven and filled the whole house where they were sitting. They saw what seemed to be tongues of fire that separated and came to rest on each of them. All of them were filled with the Holy Spirit and began to speak in other tongues as the Spirit enabled them.' **ACTS 2:1–4**

Jesus had promised His team that He would send a Coach to help them. A Coach who would motivate, train and get them working as a team. Someone who would give them the skills and power they needed in the struggle for the world championships.

On the holiday feast of Pentecost, the whole squad met together. God chose this opportunity to introduce the Coach He had promised. And what a **DRAMATIC FIRST IMPRESSION** He made on the team. Talk about firing them up. The team of no-hopers were immediately turned into a world championship winning side. So who was this Coach?

God the Holy Spirit had come to live inside each of the players. Wherever they went they had their own Personal Coach to get them **PERFORMING GOD'S WAY.**

And, if they fouled it up, their Personal Coach was there to show them where they had gone wrong and to correct them. God living in them made such a difference to the team.

>ENGAGE

We have the same Personal Coach today – God the Holy Spirit. He loves to fill our lives and get us moving forward for God. He coaches us in how to support others and work as part of a team. He misses us when we sit on the sidelines or skive off training. So are you listening to your Personal Coach? Are you working with Him to improve your skills? Ask God to fill you with the Holy Spirit so you can bring glory to Him by the way you play your life.

TEAM MORALE

'They devoted themselves to the apostles' teaching and to fellowship, to the breaking of bread and to prayer. Everyone was filled with awe at the many wonders and signs performed by the apostles. All the believers were together and had everything in common. They sold property and possessions to give to anyone who had need. Every day they continued to meet together in the temple courts. They broke bread in their homes and ate together with glad and sincere hearts, praising God and enjoying the favour of all the people. And the Lord added to their number daily those who were being saved.' **ACTS 2:42–47**

God the Holy Spirit introduced a completely new formation to the team. There were no superstars for a start. God the Holy Spirit coached the squad to perform just as Jesus had done. There were no prima donnas – everyone was trained to support each other. There were no stars demanding better pay – the team shared all their possessions and gave to those in need.

Each person realised how important it was to train each day by praying, learning God's tactics for living and remembering what Jesus had done for them.

They attended their team meetings in the Temple to worship God. **TEAM MORALE WAS HIGH.** They socialised together in the evenings. Others were impressed by the team spirit in the side. **EVERY DAY MORE PEOPLE BELIEVED THAT JESUS WAS ALIVE,** so they wanted some of what the team had and signed on too!

>ENGAGE

So are you pleased to be a member of Jesus' all-time world championship squad? Isn't it great to be on a side that knows they will become champions! Tell God what you have learnt about being a member of His team and ask for His help to put it all into action. God wants you to be on the ball for Him.

DON'T GIVE IN
THIS WAY OUT

'This, then, is how you should pray:
"Our Father in heaven,
hallowed be your name,
your kingdom come,
your will be done,
on earth as it is in heaven.
Give us today our daily bread.
And forgive us our debts,
as we also have forgiven our debtors.
And lead us not into temptation,
but deliver us from the evil one."
For if you forgive other people when
they sin against you, your heavenly
Father will also forgive you. But if you do
not forgive others their sins, your Father
will not forgive your sins.' **MATTHEW 6:9–15**

Today we start looking at the theme of temptation. Don't run away! I know **IT'S A TOUGH SUBJECT, BUT IT'S AN IMPORTANT ONE** so let's stick with it! We all face temptation at some point in our life; sometimes it feels like a constant stream of it from TV, the internet, our mates and modern culture.

To be prepared we must first understand what temptation is. Temptation is not sin. It's a thought or desire, or an appeal to us, to do something that's against God's will. The out of order thoughts and ideas are not sin.

They become sin when we act on them – either by welcoming and 'feeding' them in our minds, or by actually doing them. You can't stop a bird flying over your head but you can stop it making a nest in your hair. Jesus taught His disciples to ask God to rescue them from the evil one – Satan. He saw it as being so important to resist that temptation was included in the Lord's Prayer. The enemy of God does all he can to divert our attention from God and His plans. So it's important we use our direct line to God for help when we are tempted to step out of line.

>ENGAGE

Satan is out to cut you off from God, and sin is the one thing that will separate you from God. Don't be fooled by Satan's tricks.

Stay close to God. You can't just say, 'God, lead me not into temptation' – your words need to become actions: PRAYER+ACTIONS=RESISTANCE!!

At some point today, pray the Lord's Prayer – not just reciting it off by heart as you may have done in the past – but really praying it *in* your heart.

FREE TO MESS UP

'When tempted, no one should say, "God is tempting me." For God cannot be tempted by evil, nor does he tempt anyone; but each person is tempted when they are dragged away by their own evil desire and enticed. Then, after desire has conceived, it gives birth to sin; and sin, when it is full-grown, gives birth to death. Don't be deceived, my dear brothers and sisters. Every good and perfect gift is from above, coming down from the Father of the heavenly lights, who does not change like shifting shadows.' **JAMES 1:13–17**

Let's look at who and what we need to steer clear of, according to the Bible.

God sometimes allows us to be tempted to test our trust in Him, but **GOD NEVER EVER TEMPTS US.** He would never deceive us into doing wrong.

Temptation grabs us from three directions: from inside (our thoughts and desires), from around us (people encouraging us to do wrong) and directly from Satan. The problem occurs because God gave us minds that are **FREE TO MAKE CHOICES.** God didn't want us to be mindless robots programmed to carry out His wishes. He made us so we could choose to obey Him, which also means we can choose to disobey.

It's God's nature never to force His will on us. So as long as we have a choice, there will always be temptation. But only when we side with God will we grow as Christians, for resisting temptation builds the character of Jesus in us.

>ENGAGE God is waiting to help us in our struggles. He wants to show us where we are being tricked into accepting less than the best in our lives. He wants us to make a deliberate choice for Him and to enjoy His good and perfect gifts. So talk with Him and ask for His support in resisting temptation.

HE'S BEEN THERE

'Therefore, since we have a great high priest who has ascended into heaven, Jesus the Son of God, let us hold firmly to the faith we profess. For we do not have a high priest who is unable to feel sympathy for our weaknesses, but we have one who has been tempted in every way, just as we are – yet he did not sin. Let us then approach God's throne of grace with confidence, so that we may receive mercy and find grace to help us in our time of need.' **HEBREWS 4:14–16**

Temptation shows us a door labelled 'way in'. But there is another option if you look for it – 'way out'. Which route did Jesus take when He was tempted?

Jesus experienced all the hassles and trials of life and was severely tempted to opt out of God's plans for His life, but He stuck with them even when it meant crucifixion. Again, this underlines that sin and temptation are not the same thing. **JESUS WAS TEMPTED BUT DID NOT SIN.** When shown the 'way in' door, He turned for the exit.

Some Christians feel guilty because they're tempted, even though they never proceed from thought to action. There is no reason for them to be guilty if the initial thought was identified as wrong and resisted. But didn't

Jesus say that if we think lustful thoughts about someone it is a sin (Matt. 5:27–28)? Well, the issue here is what we do with the temptation. If the wrong desire comes and we resist it, we obey God. If we welcome it and spend time thinking about it, then we go against God's plans to keep our minds clean.

Remember, you are not guilty because you are tempted – **IT'S THE 'SECOND LOOK' SYNDROME THAT'S THE SIN.**

>ENGAGE

When tempted, don't linger or open the 'way in' door to glimpse what's on offer. Turn away and look for the way out. This is particularly hard when you're in a group that doesn't care what God thinks about their actions. Talk with Jesus. He's overcome every temptation you will ever face in the power of the Holy Spirit.

PRAY

Jesus, thank You for understanding what temptation feels like. Please help me not to give in when temptation strikes. Amen.

THE DOOR'S OPEN

'These things happened to them as examples and were written down as warnings for us, on whom the culmination of the ages has come. So, if you think you are standing firm, be careful that you don't fall! No temptation has overtaken you except what is common to mankind. And God is faithful; he will not let you be tempted beyond what you can bear. But when you are tempted, he will also provide a way out so that you can endure it.' **1 CORINTHIANS 10:11–13**

A way out can be found. The worst thing about being in Colditz (the most secure Second World War prison camp) was knowing that no one had ever escaped. But when word spread that escape was possible, half the problems of morale and hopelessness were overcome.

God makes a brilliant promise to Christians. When you're tempted, He always opens an escape route for you. You are never trapped unless you want to be. It's vital to realise that *THERE IS ALWAYS A WAY OUT.* The problem Paul highlights is that we often get lulled into thinking we are living OK as a Christian and won't be controlled by any serious temptations. Beware!

JUST WHEN YOU THINK YOU HAVE GOT YOUR ACT TOGETHER YOU'RE MOST LIKELY TO GET CAUGHT.

Remember this – God will never allow you to be tempted beyond your ability to resist. So, if you're 'seized' by a wrong desire, it cannot overpower you and force you to give in. We all struggle with temptation, but with God on our side we can break free.

>ENGAGE

Think of the temptations that have a strong hold on you. What escape routes has God opened? Is it to avoid going where you get tempted? Or to get rid of the things that stir up unhelpful stuff? Or to choose close friends who help rather than hinder you? The first step in finding God's escape routes is to tell Him you need His help.

ESCAPE PLAN

'Submit yourselves, then, to God. Resist the devil, and he will flee from you. Come near to God and he will come near to you. Wash your hands, you sinners, and purify your hearts, you double-minded. Grieve, mourn and wail. Change your laughter to mourning and your joy to gloom. Humble yourselves before the Lord, and he will lift you up.' **JAMES 4:7–10**

James has a great plan for finding the way out.

It's an amazing escape plan, but the trouble is we usually get this one back to front. We resist the devil – and the fight is on. 'I will not do that … I must resist …' And before you know it … 'Rats! I've messed up again …' You are doing what you didn't want to do even though you really really tried not to. So what went wrong?

Read verse 7 again. First we must submit to God, then we can resist. *IF WE TRY TO DEAL WITH THE ENEMY ON OUR OWN WE'RE SUNK.* Instead, go to God and tell Him you are struggling (He knows anyway). Do this every day – we're always gonna struggle. It's far better to keep 'short accounts' with God than to go to God at the end of a year and spend three days on your knees 'cos you've got so much to say. Let God deal with the temptation. That doesn't mean we have nothing to do. In fact we often have a lot to do, sorting out our priorities, getting into the Bible, talking with God and meeting up with other Christians. But **WITH GOD IN CONTROL OF OUR LIVES WE CAN RESIST TEMPTATION** from a position of strength.

>ENGAGE

If you have a particular problem, talk with God about it right now and allow Him to help. Where temptation is concerned He can turn our willpower into won't power. You may want to talk to a youth worker or parent about some of the areas you're struggling with.

PRAY

Father, help me to give every part of my life to You, especially the bits I struggle with. Help me to do what's right, in Your strength. Amen.

SUBMIT/RESIST

'The devil led him to Jerusalem and had him stand on the highest point of the temple. "If you are the Son of God," he said, "throw yourself down from here. For it is written:

'He will command his angels concerning you to guard you carefully; they will lift you up in their hands, so that you will not strike your foot against a stone.'"

Jesus answered, "It is said: 'Do not put the Lord your God to the test.'"

When the devil had finished all this tempting, he left him until an opportune time.' **LUKE 4:9–13**

How did Jesus avoid being tricked or trapped into doing things that were not what God wanted?

When He was tempted, Jesus didn't wrestle Satan to the ground and tell him to get lost. First **HE SUBMITTED TO GOD,** then He resisted Satan – just as James says.

How did Jesus submit Himself to God? When He was tempted to disobey, He knew Bible verses reflecting God's view on the matter. When Satan offered Jesus the world if He worshipped him, **JESUS DIDN'T GET CARRIED AWAY** imagining how great it would be to be world champion. Instead He immediately asked the question – what has God said about that? And the answer was Deuteronomy 6:13 – a verse that most six-year-old Jewish boys knew by heart: 'Fear the LORD your God, serve him only and take your oaths in his name.'

It's incredibly difficult to resist temptation by fighting it … it's impossible by ignoring it – because it always returns. The thought or desire needs to be replaced with God's thoughts on the matter (Phil. 4:8).

>ENGAGE

Think of the areas where you struggle with temptation. What Bible verses explain God's opinion on the way you should behave? Learn these verses and repeat them when you need help in saying 'no' to wrong.

PRAY

Lord, help me to know Your Word and understand it better, so that I can tell Satan to get lost. Amen.

RUN AWAY!

'Flee the evil desires of youth and pursue righteousness, faith, love and peace, along with those who call on the Lord out of a pure heart. Don't have anything to do with foolish and stupid arguments, because you know they produce quarrels. And the Lord's servant must not be quarrelsome but must be kind to everyone, able to teach, not resentful.'

2 TIMOTHY 2:22–24

There is a way out of temptation. So what do you do? Stay where you are or run for your life? Here's what Paul told young Timothy to do.

'Flee' means: don't just stand there, get out, and quickly! Don't hang around in a situation that causes you difficulties – make a U-turn. *RUN AWAY FROM TEMPTATION, NOT TOWARDS IT.*

Stay clear of the top shelf in the newsagent's, don't watch that film, turn off the TV, avoid that troublesome group of people. If it's a particular person who's causing you problems – don't get too closely involved.

Why does Paul tell us to get out of the danger zone? Simply because disobedience has consequences and nobody gets away with breaking God's ground rules. Don't cause yourself and others a lot of unnecessary hurt and aggravation by hanging around in a 'no-go' area to sample the action.

>ENGAGE

God has a getaway vehicle ready and revved up to get us out of temptation before it is too late. Our problem is that we often don't want to quit the scene. If you really want to live for God, ask Him to give you a 'flee in the ear' reminder when you stray into one of His forbidden areas.

RESISTANCE

'An angry person stirs up conflict, and a hot-tempered person commits many sins. Pride brings a person low, but the lowly in spirit gain honour.

The accomplices of thieves are their own enemies; they are put under oath and dare not testify.

Fear of man will prove to be a snare, but whoever trusts in the LORD is kept safe.

Many seek an audience with a ruler, but it is from the LORD that one gets justice.

The righteous detest the dishonest; the wicked detest the upright.'

PROVERBS 29:22–27

Why is it that we can resist everything except temptation? Why don't we back out of the situation and stay free? One reason is that others put us under pressure … to stay on the wrong path.

'Go on, it's only a bit of fun …' 'Everybody else is doing it …' Others often put us under pressure to do things which bring God's disapproval. **IT IS VERY DIFFICULT TO SAY NO** because we don't want to be thought of as a wimp or a member of the 'God squad'. We sometimes have a deep fear of being thought of as an oddball if we refuse to drift along with the crowd when they are heading out of bounds.

We often face the choice of going off the rails with our mates or **KEEPING ON THE RIGHT TRACK WITH GOD.** So whose approval do you want most?

It's harder to say 'NO' than it is to go with the flow. You're a bigger man if you can resist and stand up for what you believe. Don't let other humans control your life – put God in the driving seat.

>ENGAGE Are you being put under pressure at the moment to do things which you know displease God? Ask God to help you become more concerned about Him.

PRAY

Father, help me when following You means going against the flow. I want to please You first and foremost, not my mates. Amen.

CAPTAIN JOSH
FEARSOME

'So Joshua fought the Amalekites as Moses had ordered, and Moses, Aaron and Hur went to the top of the hill. As long as Moses held up his hands, the Israelites were winning, but whenever he lowered his hands, the Amalekites were winning. When Moses' hands grew tired, they took a stone and put it under him and he sat on it. Aaron and Hur held his hands up – one on one side, one on the other – so that his hands remained steady till sunset. So Joshua overcame the Amalekite army with the sword.' **EXODUS 17:10–13**

▶ Let's move on to looking at a key figure in the Old Testament – Joshua, and importantly – what God had in store for him.

NAME// The name Joshua means 'the Lord's salvation'. His name is inscribed on Egyptian tablets made at the time of the Israelites' conquest of Canaan.

RANK// Captain.

BACKGROUND// He was the son of Nun. That doesn't mean he didn't have parents or that his mother was Catholic – Nun was his family surname.

PROSPECTS// There is Nun better than Joshua for showing courage and trust in God.

The Israelites were a tough bunch. Years of pumping iron as slaves in Egypt left them with bulging biceps and pumped up pectorals. And ***NONE WERE***

TOUGHER than the man they chose to lead them into battle – Captain Josh.

Joshua the battling Nun was chosen to lead the Israelites into their first conflict for over 400 years. And although he was a fearsome fighter, he learnt a great lesson that day. **NO MATTER HOW BIG AND TOUGH YOU ARE, WITHOUT GOD'S HELP YOU'RE A LOSER.** Only when Moses held his hands up in prayer to God could Joshua force the Amalekites to retreat.

God asked Moses to write a note to Joshua after the battle. It read, 'The Lord will terminate the Amalekites. You don't have to worry about them.'

>ENGAGE

When we battle against temptation or difficulties we are sometimes forced to retreat in fear of failure. Joshua was overpowered when he didn't have prayer support. So why not talk with God about any tough situations you are up against and enlist His help? He'll show you how to square up to difficulties and make progress.

PRAY

Father, thank You that You know all about me. Help me to ask for Your advice, and then to take it in all situations in my life. Amen.

BEING MENTORED

'As Moses went into the tent, the pillar of cloud would come down and stay at the entrance, while the LORD spoke with Moses. Whenever the people saw the pillar of cloud standing at the entrance to the tent, they all stood and worshipped, each at the entrance to their tent. The LORD would speak to Moses face to face, as one speaks to a friend. Then Moses would return to the camp, but his young assistant Joshua son of Nun did not leave the tent.' **EXODUS 33:9–11**

Pitched outside the Israelite camp was a tent where Moses went to talk with God. They talked face to face, just as you would talk to a friend. And one man was privileged enough to get to listen in to their conversations – Captain Josh.

Moses took Joshua away from the camp to learn how to talk with God. He let the young man listen in as he spoke with God about national and personal issues.

Earlier, Moses had taken Joshua with him as he climbed Mount Sinai to learn God's rules for living. Joshua was only allowed halfway up the mountain, but Moses climbed to the summit to speak with God. From this position Joshua drew Moses' attention to the noise the disobedient Israelites were making as they got drunk, behaved wildly and worshipped a golden calf.

IT WAS A TOUGH SITUATION FOR JOSHUA AT TIMES. Outside the camp, or halfway up the mountain, he was able to steer clear of the trouble his mates sometimes got into, but it could be lonely. He didn't yet enjoy the close relationship that Moses enjoyed with God. But by being where God wanted, when God wanted, **HE LEARNT HOW TO LISTEN TO GOD AND TAKE HIS ADVICE.**

>ENGAGE

Do you sometimes feel left out? You're not enjoying a 'mountain top' experience with God and you're not joining in the wild times with everyone else. Like Joshua you're stuck in the middle. Don't worry! Use this time to build a closer relationship with God. Learn to talk with Him and get His advice. And in time you will experience the amazing benefits that close friendship with God adds to your life.

PRAY

Father, thank You that You are always there for me. Help me to trust You and follow You. Amen.

DON'T BOTTLE OUT

'I will give you every place where you set your foot, as I promised Moses. Your territory will extend from the desert to Lebanon, and from the great river, the Euphrates – all the Hittite country – to the Mediterranean Sea in the west. No one will be able to stand against you all the days of your life. As I was with Moses, so I will be with you; I will never leave you nor forsake you. Be strong and courageous, because you will lead these people to inherit the land I swore to their ancestors to give them.' **JOSHUA 1:3–6**

Forty years after leading the Israelites into battle for the first time, Joshua was poised for action at the border of Canaan. Moses, their great leader, was dead and Joshua was now in charge.

On an earlier spying mission Joshua had noted the military might of the inhabitants of Canaan, but was convinced that **WITH GOD'S HELP THEY COULD TAKE THE LAND.** Now God was giving him the chance to put his faith into action.

God promised to give Joshua all the land he stepped on from the desert to the Med, which meant he had to charge forward in his size 10 sandals trusting God that he would not come unstuck in the land of milk and honey.

God gave Joshua the secret of success: **LEARN GOD'S WORD, THINK ABOUT GOD'S WORD, OBEY GOD'S WORD** – not just the parts you like, all of it!

God also gave Joshua a good reason why he should never bottle out of a battle. He would be with him just as He had been with Moses, and would never let him down.

>ENGAGE

The Word of God is not just a text book, a rule book or a story book. Somehow, mysteriously, through the Holy Spirit, the life and character of God are contained within it. The more time we spend reading it and obeying it, the more that life comes to be shown in our own bodies and character. The New Testament says that Jesus was the Word of God in human form. Ask God to make you more like Jesus as you read His Word.

UP THE WALL

'When they left, they went into the hills and stayed there three days, until the pursuers had searched all along the road and returned without finding them. Then the two men started back. They went down out of the hills, forded the river and came to Joshua son of Nun and told him everything that had happened to them. They said to Joshua, "The LORD has surely given the whole land into our hands; all the people are melting in fear because of us."' **JOSHUA 2:22–24**

Ten of the 12 spies who first went into Canaan wanted out of God's plans. Only Joshua and Caleb wanted to invade. Forty years later, with Joshua in charge, another spying mission was underway to get an update on the situation.

The daring spies found a way into the fortified city of Jericho. Rahab, a woman with a house built into the city wall, often entertained travellers. When Rahab realised she was harbouring Israelite spies, she didn't betray them. Why? Well, news of the way God had led the Israelites through the Red Sea had reached Jericho. People in the city were afraid of God – really petrified!

THEY WERE PREPARING FOR SIEGE,

but Rahab knew the only way to be saved was to ask God for mercy. The spies agreed to spare Rahab and her family when they returned to attack the city.

The news that the people of Jericho were up the wall with fear was great news for Joshua. **GOD WAS ALREADY FIGHTING FOR THEM.**

>ENGAGE

Rahab had a bad reputation in the city for her immoral lifestyle. God had a high reputation in the city for the way He had led the Israelites to victory. Yet God was willing to spare Rahab's life when she asked for mercy. Thank God for the forgiveness He has shown us. Instead of bringing us down, He wants to lift us up.

PRAY

Father, thank You for Your willingness to forgive us if we ask and for providing a way for us to receive Your forgiveness by sending Jesus. Amen.

OVER THE RIVER

CAPTAIN JOSH

'Joshua told the people, "Consecrate yourselves, for tomorrow the LORD will do amazing things among you."

Joshua said to the priests, "Take up the ark of the covenant and pass on ahead of the people." So they took it up and went ahead of them.

And the LORD said to Joshua, "Today I will begin to exalt you in the eyes of all Israel, so that they may know that I am with you as I was with Moses."' **JOSHUA 3:5–8**

The River Jordan was the first border the Israelites needed to cross to enter Canaan. No one expected them to attempt a crossing at harvest time because the river was in flood. But God is the God of surprises.

God didn't sort things out for the Israelites until they had done all He asked them. Everyone had to pack their suitcases and label them for the Promised Land. They had a day to *GET THEMSELVES RIGHT WITH GOD* and renew their trust in Him. Then they had to follow the priests carrying the ark towards the flooded river. Nothing happened. But then God had not promised anything would happen until the priests leading the procession dipped their toes in the water.

The priests (without a raft or bridge) *STEPPED FORWARD IN FAITH,* carrying the heavy ark.

If God didn't act, they would sink into the water under the weight of the ark. But as they stepped in, God stepped in to take the river out in one hit. Over a million people crossed the Jordan without so much as a wet sandal.

And where was God while they crossed? The ark of God was held high in the middle of the dry river bed and remained there until the last crossing. God is always where we need Him, when we need Him.

>ENGAGE

Where is God when we need Him? Right in the middle of the difficulty we face, ready to help stop us getting swept away. All we need to do is head in the direction God wants us to go. Spend time with God getting ready to face the day ahead and get into action doing the things He has asked you to do. You never know what amazing things might happen.

POWERFUL

'In the future when your descendants ask ... "What do these stones mean?" tell them, "Israel crossed the Jordan on dry ground." For the LORD your God dried up the Jordan before you until you had crossed over. The LORD your God did to the Jordan what he had done to the Red Sea when he dried it up before us until we had crossed over. He did this so that all the peoples of the earth might know that the hand of the LORD is powerful and so that you might always fear the LORD your God.' **JOSHUA 4:21–24**

God held back the River Jordan 18 miles upstream at a place called Adam. As the Israelites crossed over, one man from each tribe was chosen to pick up a large stone from the river bed and carry it to their new campsite at Gilgal.

No sooner had the last person crossed the dry river bed than the flood waters surged down the valley again. Twice last century the collapse of cliffs at Adam has blocked the river, once for more than 21 hours. God caused a blockage that was exactly timed between the first and last person crossing the Jordan.

The Israelites didn't show passports at the border crossing, but they had something to declare –

THE LORD IS POWERFUL! They arranged the 12 stones collected from the dry river bed into a monument to remind future generations how God had got them into the Promised Land.

Joshua, who risked being thought of as a fool had God not stopped the river, earned great respect as a leader. **GOD WAS UNDOUBTEDLY WITH HIM** just as He had been with Moses.

>ENGAGE

The Lord is powerful! We know that, but we need to be reminded. God asked Joshua to pile up 12 stones at Gilgal because He knows how quickly we forget His power. Remember some of the things God has done for you. Praise God and give Him thanks!

PREPARING FOR WAR

'See, I have delivered Jericho into your hands, along with its king and its fighting men. March round the city once with all the armed men. Do this for six days. Make seven priests carry trumpets of rams' horns in front of the ark. On the seventh day, march round the city seven times, with the priests blowing the trumpets. When you hear them sound a long blast on the trumpets, make the whole army give a loud shout; then the wall of the city will collapse and the army will go up, everyone straight in.' **JOSHUA 6:2–5**

Blocking the Israelites' progress into the Promised Land was the walled city of Jericho, the **OLDEST INHABITED CITY KNOWN TO MAN.** Joshua had never laid siege to a fortified city before. Was it time to build siege ramps, ladders and battering rams?

Joshua made some very strange preparations for war. God had promised the land of Canaan to Abraham and his descendants on the condition that all the Israelite males were circumcised. But the present Israelites had not kept their part in the deal. So the Lord told them to put this matter right before they went into battle. No gain without pain, as they say!

They also celebrated how God had led them out of Egypt by having a Passover meal. The next day it was 'What's this? There's no *what's this*!' God had stopped His daily bread round of manna (the word 'manna' means 'what's this?'). They now had the choice of a full takeaway menu with a chef's special of milk and honey.

Once Joshua and the Israelites had sorted themselves out with God, they learnt that Jericho wouldn't be a problem – they could walk it. **PROVIDING THEY FOLLOWED GOD'S BATTLE PLANS** it would take just 13 rounds to blast the walls down.

>ENGAGE

Sometimes we battle on against temptation or difficulties without making progress, so it's good to check out our lives and get into the habit of meeting up with God and other Christians on a regular basis. Take time at church to listen and talk with your youth group about what you've heard, and you may start to get to know God better. Getting closer to God will help you to understand Him more, and also helps in learning how to overcome tough obstacles His way and not ours.

THE WALLS COME DOWN

'The seventh time round, when the priests sounded the trumpet blast, Joshua commanded the army, "Shout! For the LORD has given you the city! The city and all that is in it are to be devoted to the LORD ... But keep away from the devoted things, so that you will not bring about your own destruction by taking any of them. Otherwise you will make the camp of Israel liable to destruction and bring trouble on it."' **JOSHUA 6:16–18**

Hundreds of years before Joshua arrived on the scene, Jericho had thick city walls guarded by high stone towers and an enormous ditch cut in the rock. God's strategy of firing on all seven trumpets seemed totally off the wall.

God intended to bring Jericho down because its inhabitants were wicked. Strict instructions were given that no one was to take any of the idols or treasures in the city.

Why did God bring the walls down in this way? First, to teach the Israelites that *YOU WIN BATTLES BY OBEYING GOD* to the last detail. Second, you win battles by blowing God's trumpet, not your own.

Joshua and his troops didn't get the medals for this campaign – **THE GLORY WENT TO GOD.** Strangely enough, by obeying God and honouring Him Joshua earned great respect as a soldier, not only among his troops but also among his enemies (see Josh. 6:27).

Did you notice that the Israelite spies kept their promise and spared Rahab and her family? God keeps His promises and we should keep ours.

>ENGAGE

What can we learn from this battle? Well, no problem is too difficult for God to overcome. It's also important that we spend each day quietly doing what God wants – reading the Bible, talking with Him and carrying out His instructions, no matter how ridiculous we might feel. When we keep in step with God each day it's not long before He gives us something to really shout about. Ask God today what He wants you to do, and dare to do it!

FACE UP

'Israel has sinned; they have violated my covenant, which I commanded them to keep. They have taken some of the devoted things; they have stolen, they have lied, they have put them with their own possessions. That is why the Israelites cannot stand against their enemies; they turn their backs and run because they have been made liable to destruction. I will not be with you any more unless you destroy whatever among you is devoted to destruction.'
JOSHUA 7:11–12

Just when you think you are a winner for God, you go and blow it. Know what I mean? It is so easy to get involved with wrong stuff because we think we can conceal it from others. God spotted something during the battle of Jericho that no one else saw, and brought the Israelites down to earth with a bang.

What went wrong at Ai? Joshua needed to capture this city so he could take control of the moorland plateau north of Jerusalem. What a disaster! Thirty-six men dead and 3,000 of his crack troops sent packing by a bunch of no-hopers. God hadn't fought with them! But why?

Someone had broken their promise not to steal idols or treasures from Jericho. He had been careful to conceal his bounty, forgetting that **GOD KNOWS EVERYTHING.**

Morale sank because morals had sunk. The Israelites learnt that they would never defeat their enemies while they were sneakily disobeying God. They needed to **FACE UP TO THEIR FAILURE** and deal with the matter immediately.

God cannot fight for us when we are fighting against Him.

We can fool some of the people some of the time, but we can never fool God. Disobedience quenches the power of the Holy Spirit and leaves us defeated and discouraged. So if you're losing out as a Christian, ask yourself, 'What's going on here? Is there something wrong in my life that God needs to deal with before I can enjoy His power and victory?' Talk it through with God. That's what Joshua did.

BURIED IN THE SAND

'Then Joshua said to Achan, "My son, give glory to the LORD, the God of Israel, and honour him. Tell me what you have done; do not hide it from me."

Achan replied, "It is true! I have sinned against the LORD, the God of Israel. This is what I have done: when I saw in the plunder a beautiful robe from Babylonia, two hundred shekels of silver and a bar of gold weighing fifty shekels, I coveted them and took them. They are hidden in the ground inside my tent, with the silver underneath."' **JOSHUA 7:19–21**

So who was the culprit who had looted Jericho? Who'd found trouble in the rubble? God was about to uncover a can of worms (or should I say Achan of worms) lurking beneath the surface.

The whole of Israel stood in an identity parade. By a process of elimination **GOD EXPOSED ACHAN** as the thief. He confessed to shoplifting a top-of-the-range designer coat and several thousand pounds of cash. A search of his premises led to the stolen goods being recovered.

Achan had buried the loot in the sand – along with his head. He really thought he would get away with it. God had given everyone 24 hours to own up, but Achan kept quiet. As the net closed on him he didn't come forward. Only when he was arrested did he confess.

Achan's **GREED AND DECEIT RESULTED IN TROUBLE** for him, trouble for his family, trouble for Joshua and trouble for the Israelites. In fact, the area was renamed the Valley of Trouble.

Nothing has changed. Disobedience has a shadow called trouble. The two are inseparable. Invite one into your life and you invite both.

>ENGAGE

Think about how disobedience can get us into trouble today. How do people try to conceal their guilt? What does God want us to do when we land ourselves or others in trouble? Achan could have avoided trouble by keeping out of the rubble. What do you need to do to keep out of trouble? Ask God for help. Maybe chat to some Christian friends about it, and then pray for each other and for God's help in resisting temptation.

AMBUSH!

'Then the LORD said to Joshua, "Do not be afraid; do not be discouraged. Take the whole army with you, and go up and attack Ai. For I have delivered into your hands the king of Ai, his people, his city and his land. You shall do to Ai and its king as you did to Jericho and its king, except that you may carry off their plunder and livestock for yourselves. Set an ambush behind the city."' **JOSHUA 8:1–2**

Having dealt with their problem of disobedience, *GOD WAS ABLE TO SIDE WITH THE ISRAELITES* as they attacked Ai. God's strategy was to draw the enemy out of the city and then outflank them.

When the men of Ai saw the Israelites running away, they thought they were in for another easy killing. But God lured them into an ambush. Thirty thousand Israelites jumped out of the bushes behind the city to capture and destroy Ai.

Standing in the valley between Mount Ebal and Mount Gerizim was a very significant moment for the Israelites. They had a strategic foothold in the Promised Land. Years before, in the days of Moses, God had detailed what they were to do when they reached this valley (Deut. 27:12). Six tribes were to recite the benefits of obeying God while the other six recited the troubles that would result from disobedience.

Joshua chiselled God's rules for living onto stone, and then read them aloud for everyone to hear. **THERE WAS GOOD NEWS AND BAD NEWS.** Obeying God's rules would bring good news. Disobedience would invite bad news.

>ENGAGE

Jericho taught the Israelites the benefits of obeying God. Ai taught them the sad consequences of disobedience. We know it's best to obey God, but like the Israelites we need to be constantly reminded. When you're faced with temptation, ask God to remind you of the positives that come from obeying Him and the negatives that come from disobeying Him. And should you fail, put the matter right with Him. He gave Joshua a second chance to defeat Ai. And He is still the God of the second chance for us today.

PRAY

Father, thank You for all the great things that You give. Help me to know what I should do in difficult situations. Please help me to make the right choices. Thank You for always wanting what is best for me and for giving me second chances. Amen.

TRICKED AND TREATY

'The Israelites sampled their provisions but did not enquire of the LORD. Then Joshua made a treaty of peace with them to let them live, and the leaders of the assembly ratified it by oath.

Three days after they made the treaty with the Gibeonites, the Israelites heard that they were neighbours, living near them. So the Israelites set out and on the third day came to their cities: Gibeon, Kephirah, Beeroth and Kiriath Jearim. But the Israelites did not attack them, because the leaders of the assembly had sworn an oath to them by the LORD, the God of Israel.' **JOSHUA 9:14–18**

The Israelites now needed to secure the 10- by 12-mile plateau south-west of Ai. This area was controlled by the Gibeonites. Knowing they were **NEXT ON THE HIT LIST** and that God had forbidden the Israelites to make a treaty with them, the Gibeonites came up with a cunning plan.

What a bunch of con men the Gibeonites were. And Joshua, who didn't ask God what he should do, was completely taken in by them.

Having kitted themselves out at their local second-hand, or even twenty-second-hand, clothes shop, they posed as ambassadors from a country outside the Promised Land. Next they produced food and drink that was well past its sell-by date, claiming it was fresh when they set off on their journey. How did they keep a straight face?

What a bunch of smooth talkers they were too. 'We are your servants ... (grovel, grovel). We think your God is great ... (lick Joshua's sandals). He is famous in our land for the way he led you out of Egypt and defeated your enemies in the desert ... (whatever you do don't mention Jericho or they will know we are locals). We want to make a peace treaty with you (more sandal licking).'

Joshua, thinking he would have the support of a foreign power in his conquest of Canaan, agreed to a treaty **_UNDER SOLEMN OATH._** What an airhead he felt a few days later when he discovered they lived just round the corner. Although he was angry, Joshua didn't break the treaty, but made the Gibeonites into lumberjacks and water carriers for the Israelites.

Don't be fooled by appearances or words. Ask God to show you the right thing to do in each situation of your life. Be willing to ask questions and find answers. Matthew 7:7 encourages us to do this and guarantees that we will find what we are looking for.

SOS

'So Joshua marched up from Gilgal with his entire army, including all the best fighting men. The LORD said to Joshua, "Do not be afraid of them; I have given them into your hand. Not one of them will be able to withstand you."

After an all-night march from Gilgal, Joshua took them by surprise. The LORD threw them into confusion before Israel, so Joshua and the Israelites defeated them completely at Gibeon. Israel pursued them along the road going up to Beth Horon and cut them down all the way to Azekah and Makkedah.' **JOSHUA 10:7–10**

The Amorites were fearful of the Israelites advancing through the middle of their land. A coalition of armies was formed to recapture the strategic plateau of Gibeon. Joshua and his men were 20 miles away in Gilgal when the Amorites tried to nail the Gibeonites.

The besieged Gibeonites sent an SOS to Joshua, who was still getting over the fact that he had been deceived by them. But *A PROMISE IS A PROMISE* and Joshua put his feelings aside to honour the treaty. God reassured Joshua that he would give the Amorites a right 'ammering.

The Israelites made a surprise dawn raid that panicked the Amorites into retreat. They fled through the mountain pass, hoping to regroup at Azekah, 20 miles away, for a counterattack. God was not going to allow them to escape His judgment. **HE BROUGHT IN HIS HEAVY ARTILLERY** and bombarded them with hailstones – our God reigns and our God rains!

The survivors, hoping to escape under cover of darkness, also got a shock. God caused the sun and moon to stay on full beam for 24 hours. The Amorites were absolutely routed.

>ENGAGE

All sorts of amazing miracles happen in the Bible, and here we have an outstanding one. It can be tempting to get involved in endless and pointless discussions about whether these things really happened or not. The Bible tells us that God holds and sustains the whole universe moment by moment. He makes things out of nothing and brings life from death. He can do just what He wants and will always act to fulfil His plans for His people. Jesus said, 'You're either for me or against me.' If you are for Him then you can't lose, if you're against Him then you can't win – simple, huh?

PRAY

Father, thank You for making me as I am. Help me to understand more of You and Your amazing power. Amen.

SURPRISE!

'The LORD said to Joshua, "Do not be afraid of them, because by this time tomorrow I will hand all of them, slain, over to Israel. You are to hamstring their horses and burn their chariots."

So Joshua and his whole army came against them suddenly at the Waters of Merom and attacked them, and the LORD gave them into the hand of Israel. They defeated them and pursued them all the way to Greater Sidon, to Misrephoth Maim, and to the Valley of Mizpah on the east, until no survivors were left.'

JOSHUA 11:6–8

Captain Josh went on to secure the southern parts of the Promised Land. The heavily armed Canaanite warriors of the north joined forces, convinced that their horses and chariots would run down the Israelite hill fighters.

The Israelites, without metal weapons or chariots, faced a **VASTLY BETTER EQUIPPED ARMY.** But God promised a 24-hour victory delivery service.

He told Joshua to make a surprise attack on the Canaanites as they camped in the heavy sycamore and oak forests at Merom. Unable to steer their one-horse power chariots through the trees, the Canaanites fled. The Israelites fired after them, burning their chariots and the key city of Hazor. Archaeological work at Hazor in the 1920s and 1950s confirms that it was destroyed by fire at the time of Joshua (11:11). It was a centre for worship of the moon goddess.

The Israelites cut off all the escape routes and chopped down the Canaanites in the forest. **GOD WON THE DAY – IN A DAY!**

>ENGAGE

God let the Israelites win as hill fighters. He didn't expect them to get kitted up with the latest battle gear to match the Canaanites. Sometimes we're jealous of those who look good and act self-assured, and we may try to dress or act like them. But there is a danger they might lead us into trouble. Remember there's no need to try and be someone God doesn't want you to be.

PRAY

Father, again, thank You for making me be me. Help me to remember that You made me for a reason. Amen.

RESCUE

"'Now then, just as the LORD promised, he has kept me alive for forty-five years since the time he said this to Moses, while Israel moved about in the wilderness. So here I am today, eighty-five years old!" ... Then Joshua blessed Caleb son of Jephunneh and gave him Hebron as his inheritance ... Not one of all the LORD's good promises to Israel failed; every one was fulfilled.'

JOSHUA 14:10–13; 21:45

Remember Caleb? He was one of the original 12 spies Moses sent into Canaan. Of the 12, only he and Joshua believed God could help them take the land. **AS A RESULT OF THEIR FAITH,** Caleb and Joshua were the only two people of their generation who lived to enter the land 40 years later.

Caleb was 40 years old when he reported back from his spying mission. His enthusiasm to trust God and take the land was met with stony silence then stony violence. God rescued Caleb from being stoned to death and promised that he would live to settle in Canaan.

Caleb crossed the Jordan as an 80-year-old. Did he head for the first nursing home and apply for a free bus pass? Never! Caleb was **FIT, STRONG AND EAGER TO LEAD** the tribe of Judah. He was in there, giving his all in every battle to secure the Promised Land.

Moses had promised to give Caleb and his descendants the hill country of Hebron, inhabited by the terrifying overgrown Anakites. Caleb was 85 years old when that promise was fulfilled. It was still inhabited by gigantic Anakites, but Caleb laid into them with his walking stick and expelled them. The geriatric General wasn't ever afraid to act on God's promises.

>ENGAGE Joshua 21:45 is a great tribute to God. The Israelites (who had spent years in the wilderness moaning and complaining to God) make a startling discovery – God had kept every one of His promises to them! Yes, every single one! And God still keeps His promises to us today – and every day. Ask God to share some of His promises for your life with you today. Dare to believe them.

SPEAK OUT

'Now that the LORD your God has given them rest as he promised, return to your homes in the land that Moses the servant of the LORD gave you on the other side of the Jordan. But be very careful to keep the commandment and the law that Moses the servant of the LORD gave you: to love the LORD your God, to walk in obedience to him, to keep his commands, to hold fast to him and to serve him with all your heart and with all your soul.' **JOSHUA 22:4–5**

Two and a half tribes had been given land to the west of Jordan, but they crossed the river to help the other tribes in their battles for Canaan. It was now time for them to return and Joshua addresses them at their passing out parade.

Joshua stands before a super macho platoon of battle hardened commandos with 31 campaign medals pinned to their chests. Their families are with them. Is Joshua puffing on a cigar, making a victory sign to the cheering crowds? 'Never in the history of hill fighting has so much been owed by so many to so few'? No, Joshua reminds them of the secret of their success.

'Attention! Keep God's commands! Get in line with His plans for you! March in step with His ways. No about turns! Love Him with all your heart and soul.'

Joshua was **NEVER AFRAID TO SPEAK OF THE LOVE OF GOD** and the need to obey Him. It made a deep impression on these macho men and when they returned home the first thing they did was to build an altar and worship God.

>ENGAGE

Never in the history of human conflict has so much been owed by so many to the Lord Jesus. Are you prepared to tell others about the love of Jesus? Joshua was never afraid to give God the credit in public. Jesus is the secret to your success, but He is a secret you can share!

PRAY

Lord Jesus, give me the courage to tell other people about You. Never let me forget to give You the credit You deserve. Amen.

PEACE TALKS

'Then Reuben, Gad and the half-tribe of Manasseh replied to the heads of the clans of Israel: "The Mighty One, God, the LORD! The Mighty One, God, the LORD! He knows! And let Israel know! If this has been in rebellion or disobedience to the LORD, do not spare us this day. If we have built our own altar to turn away from the LORD and to offer burnt offerings and grain offerings, or to sacrifice fellowship offerings on it, may the LORD himself call us to account."' **JOSHUA 22:21–23**

The two and a half tribes based west of the river Jordan had built an altar. They had done it for the best of motives, to honour God and *REMIND FUTURE GENERATIONS THAT THEY BELONGED TO HIM.* But the other tribes didn't see it like that. They suspected they were setting up a rival place of worship – and that meant war!

First there were reports of an altar the other side of the Jordan. Then there were rumours of what it might be used for. Then stories spread that these tribes were going to leave the tabernacle and set up their own worship centre. The priests felt threatened. The Israelites felt betrayed. Soldiers got armed to settle the matter by force. But no one had bothered to speak to the tribes the other side of the river and hear their point of view.

Fortunately both sides agreed to talk. And, having thrashed the matter out, they discovered there had never been a problem in the first place. The altar was a tribute to God, not a rival tabernacle. It was a reminder that **THE LORD IS GOD!** The tribes both sides of the river made peace and praised God. It was a great result.

>ENGAGE

There are all kinds of misunderstandings when people won't talk with each other. God doesn't want us to make snap judgments based on rumours, impressions and one-sided viewpoints. Such judgments cause divisions and hurt. God asks us to discern the truth – that means talking the matter through with those concerned, finding out all the facts and asking God what to do next. Discernment is motivated by love and the hope of bringing people together.

PRAY

Father, thank You that all wisdom comes from You. Please give me wisdom and patience so that I can bring people together. Amen.

FINAL WORDS

'Now fear the LORD and serve him with all faithfulness. Throw away the gods your ancestors worshipped beyond the River Euphrates and in Egypt, and serve the LORD. But if serving the LORD seems undesirable to you, then choose for yourselves this day whom you will serve, whether the gods your ancestors served beyond the Euphrates, or the gods of the Amorites, in whose land you are living. But as for me and my household, we will serve the LORD.' **JOSHUA 24:14–15**

Joshua was now an old man. Before he died he wanted to make a final broadcast to the nation. Everyone gathered to hear their great leader share *THE SECRET OF HIS SUCCESS.*

Joshua's moving speech was a tribute to God. He was not banging his own drum or trying to market his autobiography. He announced that the only reason the Canaanites had not been able to kick sand in their faces was that God had fought for them.

Captain Josh gave the nation his advice: 'Be careful to obey God, be careful to love God.' His slogan was, 'If you wanna be strong, don't do wrong.'

Then he left the nation with a choice: they could worship and obey God or they could opt for selfish lifestyles and idol worship. **_LIVING FOR GOD WOULD BRING PEACE. TURNING AWAY FROM GOD WOULD BRING TROUBLE._**

As for Josh, he had already made his choice – God first every time. He had proved in 110 years of living that it was by far the best way to live.

>ENGAGE Think of the things Joshua has taught you, and about the choice Joshua gave to God's people. What have you decided to do? Talk with God about your decision and the ways you can put it into action.

GOT ATTITUDE
GLASS HALF FULL?

'for it is God who works in you to will and to act in order to fulfil his good purpose. Do everything without grumbling or arguing, so that you may become blameless and pure, "children of God without fault in a warped and crooked generation." Then you will shine among them like stars in the sky as you hold firmly to the word of life. And then I will be able to boast on the day of Christ that I did not run or labour in vain.' **PHILIPPIANS 2:13–16**

Are you a guy with attitude? You might think that attitude means someone who is ultra cool. But we all have attitudes, thoughts and opinions that shape the way we react to the world around us. So let's get at the attitudes God wants us to have as we begin this final topic together.

You can see a glass as being **HALF EMPTY OR HALF FULL.** The facts are the same but the feelings are different. Our thoughts determine the way we react to people and situations. Just look at the two different attitudes in this passage. Some of the Christians at Philippi were moaning. Two of the women, Euodia and Syntyche, had fallen out with each other and their negative attitudes were affecting relationships in the church (Phil. 4:2).

In contrast, look at Paul, who had everything to complain about. He was a prisoner in Rome. Is he mouthing off about the food, the smell, the worry he might end up as a lion's lunch? No, he has an attitude of gratitude. He is pleased to be giving his life in the service of Jesus (Phil. 2:17).

Paul hadn't attended positive thinking classes. It was **GOD AT WORK** in him that kept him on the sunny side of the street. It was God who gave him the desire not to complain but to praise God when the going was tough. God shaped the way Paul looked at the world.

>ENGAGE

Attitudes are determined by the size of the 'i' in them. The bigger the 'i', the more self-centred our attitudes become. And when things don't work out our way then all the grouching and slouching begins. Paul learnt to put God first and be content in all situations. That's a radical change of attitude for a man who had once put the boot into Christians. God wants to make radical changes in your attitudes too.

PRAY

Lord, please help me to live Your way. Please let me see how my attitudes need to change. Amen.

ATTITUDE PROBLEMS

'For the word of God is alive and active. Sharper than any double-edged sword, it penetrates even to dividing soul and spirit, joints and marrow; it judges the thoughts and attitudes of the heart. Nothing in all creation is hidden from God's sight. Everything is uncovered and laid bare before the eyes of him to whom we must give account.' **HEBREWS 4:12–13**

Attitudes affect everything. They affect everything because they affect our relationships – with parents, friends and anyone else who happens to come along.

The trouble is that we often think it's everyone else who's got the attitude problem – not us! 'You can't be serious,' I hear you say. 'It's their fault, it's them – if only they'd ... after all I'm pretty near perfect ... most of the time ... well maybe ...' OK, how can we find out if we are stepping out of line?

When we have the Holy Spirit in our life, it is a bit like having a mirror that shows us what shape our attitudes are in. It shows if some of our attitudes are fathead-itudes. Or, if we have splat-itudes that hit out and hurt others. Or, if we use platitudes (empty statements) that look down on others.

The fact that **GOD KNOWS OUR THOUGHTS** isn't all bad news. He's not one to sit there moaning at us all the time. His motive for showing up our attitudes is so that the Holy Spirit can get to work making us more like Jesus. But **HE NEEDS OUR FULL CO-OPERATION** for that.

Remember that Jesus is sympathetic to the way we feel. He too was tempted to react with fathead-itudes, splat-itudes and platitudes, but He kept in line with God's plans for His life. He understands the pressures that put the squeeze on us. So, we can talk things through with Him at any time and ask for His help.

>ENGAGE **Would you risk a full day without looking in the mirror? No, you want to see whether you look half decent before someone else does. We spot our bad attitudes by taking a good look in the Bible. We may not like what we see, but God is able to sort us out so we can face the world in the right frame of mind.**

THE COVER-UP

'Watch out for false prophets. They come to you in sheep's clothing, but inwardly they are ferocious wolves. By their fruit you will recognise them. Do people pick grapes from thorn-bushes, or figs from thistles? Likewise, every good tree bears good fruit, but a bad tree bears bad fruit. A good tree cannot bear bad fruit, and a bad tree cannot bear good fruit. Every tree that does not bear good fruit is cut down and thrown into the fire. Thus, by their fruit you will recognise them.'

MATTHEW 7:15–20

Attitudes can't just be covered up. No matter how much you try to dunk them they have a nasty habit of popping back up to the surface.

If we're angry, the telltale signs are there in our expressions and tone of voice. If we don't like someone then it will show in our body language and the things we say about them. Whatever's inside eventually comes out.

Jesus said, 'Do people pick grapes from thorn-bushes, or figs from thistles?' The answer is obviously 'no', but the point Jesus made was very serious. ***BAD ROOT = BAD FRUIT. GOOD ROOT = GOOD FRUIT.***

Living a life that pleases God is actually what we were originally designed to do. However, you can't just sit back and let it all happen; there are things you can do to help deepen your relationship with Him. You can involve God in all areas of your life, talk to Him, read about Him and His relationship with mankind in the Bible, and allow the Holy Spirit to work in you and change you. As you begin to do these things you'll find the fruit goes from bad to good, and before you know it you'll feel like a new guy.

Jesus said this is one good way of **CHECKING PEOPLE OUT** – watch the way they behave. Does their fruit measure up against what they're teaching? People often remember your actions and forget your words.

>ENGAGE

Patience, goodness and trust in God are qualities that come to the surface when the Holy Spirit fills our inner lives. If you want to be genuine for God you'll need the help of the Holy Spirit to move your attitudes in line with Jesus. What do people remember about you?

PRAY

Holy Spirit, please fill me and change me. Let Your goodness be seen in my life. Amen.

NO BITING

'Do not repay anyone evil for evil. Be careful to do what is right in the eyes of everyone. If it is possible, as far as it depends on you, live at peace with everyone. Do not take revenge, my dear friends, but leave room for God's wrath, for it is written: "It is mine to avenge; I will repay," says the Lord.' **ROMANS 12:17–19**

A popular attitude is: when odds are against you – get even. If someone hits you then hit them back – harder! If someone insults you, return the insult.

If a dog bites you, is it sensible to bite it back? Yet when it comes to trading bad attitudes, we often slog it out to the bitter end. And it is a bitter end – revenge is never sweet. Paul told the Christians in Rome, who were receiving plenty of insults and even a few kickings, not to react tit-for-tat. Instead, they should choose to *ADOPT JESUS' ATTITUDE.* Jesus hadn't flared up but had shown love to those who mistreated Him.

God doesn't expect us to become fish-shaped punch bags, hit at from all directions and coming back for more. His advice is to get ahead, not get revenge.

How do you get ahead of someone who's treating you badly? Let God sort them out (v19). Don't react in the heat of the moment – step back and ask God to step in. God asks for room to work. He wants space and time to deal with people and situations – His way. So how can you help God? Do all you can to live at peace with people. That's not always easy if they hold grudges against you, but do all you can to smooth over the cracks. Then comes the tough bit: be kind to those who put you down. Good attitudes are powerful! **THERE'S NO SUCH THING AS GETTING EVEN.** React with bad attitudes and you lose; react with good attitudes and you win.

>ENGAGE

Under pressure, what's inside us gushes out. And when we're unfairly treated the pressure is really on. If we've got deep stores of anger and resentment they'll probably spill out. Ask the Holy Spirit to work in your life – He'll help you overcome evil with good. Chat this through with Jesus.

WHO ARE YOU TRYING TO IMPRESS?

'Therefore if you have any encouragement from being united with Christ, if any comfort from his love, if any common sharing in the Spirit, if any tenderness and compassion, then make my joy complete by being like-minded, having the same love, being one in spirit and of one mind.

Do nothing out of selfish ambition or vain conceit. Rather, in humility value others above yourselves, not looking to your own interests but each of you to the interests of the others.

In your relationships with one another, have the same mindset as Christ Jesus' **PHILIPPIANS 2:1–5**

So what's your attitude towards other Christians? Do you think they're anoraks with fish stickers? Bores with Bibles? Way past their sell-by date? Watch out – hidden attitudes don't stay hidden.

When Christians heap together for meetings you can expect someone to be climbing to the top of the pile. It happens in youth groups as well. Someone's bound to fancy themselves as God's gift to music or sport. Have you met lads who pose to impress the girls, and girls who are out to stun the lads? There may well be a few boffins boasting about their exam results and a few rebels trying to draw attention to themselves by being disruptive.

Paul asks us all to **QUESTION OUR ATTITUDES AND MOTIVES.** Who are you trying to impress? Your pals or God? Who are you trying to put in the spotlight? Yourself or Jesus? Who do you want to come out on top? Yourself or others?

Paul puts us on red alert lookout for the following ammunition which torpedoes good relationships:

SELFISH AMBITION: Flies through the air with a 'Meeeee' sound trying to make an impact.

VAIN CONCEIT: A pre-programmed missile with a big head that flattens anything in its path.

Treat people as you'd like them to treat you. Take time to get to know them. People sometimes act big in public to hide their insecurities inside. Jesus was willing to put our interests first even though it meant dying on the cross. He went down to the bottom of the pile to save us. And where did His humility take Him? To the very top of the pile. God has given Him the top spot. More about this tomorrow.

>ENGAGE

Why not pray for other Christians? Talking with God about their interests and needs will affect your attitudes towards them.

GOT ATTITUDE

'who, being in very nature God, did not consider equality with God something to be used to his own advantage; rather, he made himself nothing by taking the very nature of a servant, being made in human likeness. And being found in appearance as a man, he humbled himself by becoming obedient to death – even death on a cross!

Therefore God exalted him to the highest place and gave him the name that is above every name, that at the name of Jesus every knee should bow'

PHILIPPIANS 2:6–10

Yesterday we had the lowdown on being low. Humility is an attitude that builds good relationships. Now we get the lowdown on the ultimate 'others first' attitude – humility is cross-shaped.

'It's not fair! ... Why should I have to go? ... Why can't you do it?' Can you remember the last time you reacted like this? We like to defend what we consider to be our rights.

Suppose Jesus had reacted this way when God asked Him to come to earth and die for us? 'It's not fair! ... Why should I have to go? ... Why can't You do it?' And what if His attitude towards us had been, 'They got themselves into this mess. Why should I suffer for it?'

Jesus moved from being **THE ULTIMATE SOMEBODY TO THE ULTIMATE NOBODY.** He moved from a super rich area to a slum. He swapped adoration for insults, light for darkness, life for death. All because He put us before Himself.

To be like Jesus is to be **WILLING TO PUT OTHERS FIRST.** Not because we have to but because we genuinely care about them.

>ENGAGE

It's a crazy upside-down world! The real way of getting to the top is to give over your rights to God. The last become first and the first become last. So do you want to make it big for God? Then ask for His help in putting the needs of your parents, family, teachers, friends and others first. Remember: the way up is down.

GIVING IT ALL

'Jesus called them together and said, "You know that the rulers of the Gentiles lord it over them, and their high officials exercise authority over them. Not so with you. Instead, whoever wants to become great among you must be your servant, and whoever wants to be first must be your slave – just as the Son of Man did not come to be served, but to serve, and to give his life as a ransom for many."'

MATTHEW 20:25–28

The Bible continues to turn our attitudes upside down and inside out. Most people dream of the easy life, but Jesus opted to jump in and help others rather than lounge around in the sun.

The prophet Isaiah described the Saviour whom God would send to the world as ... a servant! This was difficult for people to understand. Why would such an important Person be a servant? Surely He would have people serving *Him*. After all, the more powerful you were the more servants you had.

The answer was that Jesus chose to serve others rather than have others serve Him. He didn't come to exploit the poor but to help them. He came as Lord, sure, but not to lord it over people. Remember how He washed His disciples' feet – a job for the lowest servant?

Jesus' attitude was one of **GIVING, NOT GETTING.** He hadn't come to grab power, money, prestige or fame. He had come to give everything He had and everything He was – even His life.

So do you expect to **BE SERVED, OR TO SERVE?** Who cleans up the mess you make around the house? Do you complain if your clothes aren't washed and ironed in time? Grumble about the meals you are cooked? Expect your parents to run a taxi service to get you around?

God wants to help us develop attitudes that are more into giving than getting. Giving your time to help around the house. Giving your best at school. If you want to make it big for God you must learn how to act like a servant, not a king.

>ENGAGE

OK. Now this is a tough one. This week really go out of your way to serve someone – do something out of the ordinary, really push the boat out to serve your family, friends, youth leaders ... anyone.

AND THE WINNER IS ...

'Then Jesus said to his disciples, "Whoever wants to be my disciple must deny themselves and take up their cross and follow me. For whoever wants to save their life will lose it, but whoever loses their life for me will find it. What good will it be for someone to gain the whole world, yet forfeit their soul? Or what can anyone give in exchange for their soul? For the Son of Man is going to come in his Father's glory with his angels, and then he will reward each person according to what they have done."'

MATTHEW 16:24–27

Be a winner and be better off! Sounds OK, but it's another upside-down, inside-out attitude. To gain – you lose. Confused? You save by losing and you lose by saving. Read it for yourself.

Matthew understood what Jesus was on about. Being a tax collector was a sure way to get rich easily, even if it meant working for the Romans and betraying fellow countrymen.

Tax collectors had a reputation for cheating and lining their own pockets by collecting more than was required and pocketing the difference. But such an attitude made a person a loser, not a winner – they lost friends, self-respect, principles – and money can't buy a place in heaven. But one day, Matthew met Jesus and it turned his world upside down (see Matt. 9:9–13).

When he decided to follow Jesus he lost his job but saved his soul. Instead of being Mr Flashy Oh-what-a-lot-I've-got of Capernaum, **HE SHARED HIS HOUSE AND MONEY** with those in need. He introduced his drinking buddies to Jesus.

Jesus helped Matthew to put self into reverse. The picture Jesus gave of someone picking up his cross was very powerful. People didn't choose to pick up a cross; they were forced to carry it on a one-way trip to crucifixion. Soon after He said this, **JESUS WILLINGLY PICKED UP HIS CROSS** to die for the sins of the world.

Picking up your cross is a picture of willingly living for God, not yourself. Matthew found it hard. He bottled out and did a runner to save his own skin when Jesus was arrested. But his attitude changed with the help of the Holy Spirit. After Pentecost, Matthew rejected the easy life to take the gospel east. The former Mr Selfish gave his life helping others to gain salvation. He won by losing!

 >ENGAGE Following God doesn't mean we think of ourselves as nobodies. It just means looking after number one takes a dive down the charts, whilst putting God first goes to the top. Following Jesus means losing but never losing out. The more we lose of our selfishness, the more we gain of God.

LIGHTEN UP

'This is the message we have heard from him and declare to you: God is light; in him there is no darkness at all. If we claim to have fellowship with him and yet walk in the darkness, we lie and do not live out the truth. But if we walk in the light, as he is in the light, we have fellowship with one another, and the blood of Jesus, his Son, purifies us from all sin.' **1 JOHN 1:5–7**

Do you look at the bright side of life or the fright side of life? Are you positive or negative about things? There are two ways of looking at anything – God's way or the wrong way.

GOD IS LIGHT. There are no dark hidden corners to His character. He's got nothing to conceal. His actions are always for our good. Satan is the very opposite – darkness. His thinking is sneaky and deceitful. His actions are negative and do us harm.

Just look how Satan's negative attitudes cloud our thinking. God promises us new life in Jesus but Satan tries to make us doubt that God even cares about us. In fact God gives us His Spirit – love, joy, peace, patience and other great, amazing gifts.

So what's the answer? Get a book on 'positive thinking'? Write out 'I'm awesome' three million times? Become an optimist? No! The secret is **ALLOWING GOD TO CHANGE US.** We need to 'walk in the light' – this simply means walking with God, allowing Him into any 'dark' or 'hidden' places in our lives. God has the power to lighten up your attitudes and brighten up your life.

>ENGAGE

Some people's attitudes are like a sweet and sour sauce. One minute they're smiling, the next they're whingeing. Talk with God if you're feeling sour about anything. It's His light that'll put a beam back on your face.

FRAMES OF MIND

GOT ATTITUDE

'There is a time for everything ... a time to weep and a time to laugh, a time to mourn and a time to dance, a time to scatter stones and a time to gather them, a time to embrace and a time to refrain from embracing ... a time to love and a time to hate, a time for war and a time for peace.' **ECCLESIASTES 3:1–8**

Life's twists and turns affect our feelings. Some situations bring sadness and it is right to weep over them. Other situations put you on top of the happy league, and it's time to celebrate. This is how the Bible puts it.

What you need to watch out for is approaching situations in the wrong frame of mind. Sometimes when you feel down, upset, flat and discouraged it's better to talk about it – even cry – rather than bottle up your sadness. But there's no excuse for becoming a full-time misery going on and on about 'poor ol' you'. A misery guts is forever holding pity parties, being moody and trying to drag others down. No wonder miseries have few friends. They grouch around trying to attract sympathy and attention. And rather than share in the happiness of others, they try and spoil the party by being miserable.

At the other extreme, **LAUGHTER IS GOD'S IDEA.** But if your attitude is to treat life as one big joke and get cheap laughs at others' expense, you're out of sync with God. Taking the rise by sinking other people is just not on.

WE NEED GOD'S HELP to be sensitive to the needs of others. Not inflicting our mood swings on them but sharing in their joys and sorrows.

>ENGAGE

Jesus partied at weddings and wept at a funeral. His attitude was right for each time. He shared in other people's happiness and comforted them in their sorrow.

PRAY

Lord Jesus, Your attitude was always right, and You were always sensitive to other people. Help me to be like this too, however I'm feeling. Amen.

OWN UP

'But if we walk in the light, as he is in the light, we have fellowship with one another, and the blood of Jesus, his Son, purifies us from all sin.
If we claim to be without sin, we deceive ourselves and the truth is not in us. If we confess our sins, he is faithful and just and will forgive us our sins and purify us from all unrighteousness. If we claim we have not sinned, we make him out to be a liar and his word is not in us.' **1 JOHN 1:7–10**

There's a new invention on the market – a pencil with an eraser at both ends. It's for people who do nothing but make mistakes.

EVERYONE MAKES MISTAKES, but not everyone likes to own up.

Some people hate to own up to their failings and will do anything to cover up. Adam and Eve's attitude, when they had chewed beyond God's limits, was to try to cover up. And that introduced a host of nasty characters called 'deception', 'lies' and 'passing the buck'.

Adam blamed Eve. Eve blamed the serpent ... No one likes taking the full rap for their mistakes, and it's tempting to blame someone else. Isn't it strange how others make stupid mistakes while we only make unavoidable errors?

In real life we all mess up. To pretend that we're faultless is a fault in itself. The differences between people show up in the way they deal with their failures. Covering up, making excuses or deflecting the blame doesn't deal with the problem. It's best to own up, **LEARN FROM OUR MISTAKES AND ASK GOD FOR HIS HELP** not to mess it up again.

It's daft to try and keep our mistakes in the dark. God says it's best to confess our sin and be sure that the blood of the Lord Jesus gives us total forgiveness. God is in the business of rubbing out our errors, not rubbing them in.

 Any time we ignore or cover up our disobedience we 'walk in darkness'. But when we bring it to light we 'walk in the light'. Our relationship with God – and others – is second rate while we try to cover our tracks. But when we come clean, God makes us clean, no matter how grubby we've got. What's your attitude towards God at this moment?

REAL PASSION

'Do not love the world or anything in the world. If anyone loves the world, love for the Father is not in them. For everything in the world – the lust of the flesh, the lust of the eyes, and the pride of life – comes not from the Father but from the world. The world and its desires pass away, but whoever does the will of God lives for ever.' **1 JOHN 2:15–17**

Our attitudes are linked to our desires. Whatever we want most controls our thinking and behaviour. So let's check out our ravings and cravings.

What may start as a wrong desire can quickly flare into a craving – a passion that overwhelms you. Getting boggle-eyed on dodgy websites or DVDs will affect your attitudes to the opposite sex. Instead of building relationships on the basis of what you can give, the high octane excitement will be in relation to what you can get. Be warned. This type of passion doesn't come from God. **WITH GOD THE EMPHASIS IS ON LOVE.** Love is kind and considerate. It doesn't boast about relationships as conquests. It isn't selfish. It doesn't delight in wrong. True love is built on trust and mutual respect. It protects people rather than exploits them. (See 1 Cor. 13:4–8.)

Some people have an attitude that causes them to boast about their over-passionate adventures and make out that you're really missing something if you don't experience the same. Are you missing out? The Bible says that **SELFISH DESIRES DON'T BRING LASTING PLEASURE.** Deep peace comes from obeying God. It's love that has the last say.

>ENGAGE

A common attitude is 'if it feels good – do it'. God's attitude is 'only if it's right – do it'. Check your attitudes to see which one you've picked up. And if you've been wandering off limits, ask God to forgive you and help you avoid situations where you'll be tempted to lose control again. God doesn't find it hard to forgive us when we really want to sort it out, but it can be hard to forgive ourselves at times.

MAKING FRIENDS

'My command is this: love each other as I have loved you. Greater love has no one than this: to lay down one's life for one's friends. You are my friends if you do what I command. I no longer call you servants, because a servant does not know his master's business. Instead, I have called you friends, for everything that I learned from my Father I have made known to you.' **JOHN 15:12–15**

Our attitudes play a big part in our friendships. The best way to get friends is to be a friend (Prov. 18:24). And there's no better example of a friendly attitude than this one.

Just take in the key attitudes of Jesus to His friends: first of all, Jesus went out of His way to choose His friends. They didn't befriend Him, He befriended them. Sometimes we need to take the initiative in getting to know people. A big smile, a friendly greeting and a willingness to find out about the things that interest them, help to build friendships. Jesus didn't only say 'hello' to fishermen Peter, Andrew, James and John – He went fishing with them.

Secondly, Jesus didn't boss others about. His disciples weren't servants, **THEY WERE HIS REAL MATES.** He shared all His plans with them. He visited their homes. He ate with them. He went on outings with them. He even flushed the dirt from between their toes before the Last Supper. Even though the disciples ran off and deserted Him, He later looked them up and made friends with them again.

Jesus has won our friendship, not by threatening or tricking us, but **BY GIVING HIS LIFE FOR US.** His great act of friendship was to put our lives before His.

 Take 'time out' and pause to think about God's great love for you. Then, as you accept and experience His love for you, it's not so hard in turn to love others.

GIVE YOUR BEST

'Slaves, obey your earthly masters with respect and fear, and with sincerity of heart, just as you would obey Christ. Obey them not only to win their favour when their eye is on you, but as slaves of Christ, doing the will of God from your heart. Serve wholeheartedly, as if you were serving the Lord, not people, because you know that the Lord will reward each one for whatever good they do, whether they are slave or free.'

EPHESIANS 6:5–8

Our attitude towards work will determine whether or not we give our best. Trying to cruise through your schoolwork or being so laid back you fall over, can mean you miss out.

When faced with work, are you more likely to break into a can of Coke than a sweat? Our attitudes are called into question in two areas:

WORKING IN GROUPS

At school, we often work together in classes and small groups. So who determines our effort? Sometimes because our pals are chatting away or messing around, we copy their attitudes rather than set the pace. No one wants to be seen as being a bit of a swot, but there are dangers if we allow others to affect our work. Try to give your best, even when those around you have switched off.

WORKING ON YOUR OWN

So what happens to your homework when there's no one nagging you to do it? Does it stay buried among the empty crisp packets in your school bag while you direct all your creative energies into making excuses? Or do you get your ballpoint rolling and give it your best shot? If we ease off when no one is putting the pressure on us to do our best, we'll never ***ACHIEVE OUR POTENTIAL.*** Paul says it's more than being self-motivated. We need to ***BE GOD-MOTIVATED*** – doing our best because we want to please Him.

>ENGAGE

If you approach your work with the attitude that you're doing it for God, you're off to a great start. It helps to be organised too. Why not make a 'To Do' list for your jobs, then work through it?

PRAY

Lord God, thank You for being interested in everything I do. Help me to remember You, whatever I'm doing. Amen.

HELP!

'The centurion replied, "Lord, I do not deserve to have you come under my roof. But just say the word, and my servant will be healed. For I myself am a man under authority, with soldiers under me. I tell this one, 'Go,' and he goes; and that one, 'Come,' and he comes. I say to my servant, 'Do this,' and he does it." When Jesus heard this, he was amazed and said to those following him, "Truly I tell you, I have not found anyone in Israel with such great faith."' **MATTHEW 8:8–10**

Jesus spotlighted one man's attitude as being an example to the nation of Israel. Who was he? Well he wasn't Jewish for a start.

When the Roman centurion in charge of the garrison in Capernaum faced a problem he couldn't handle, he went to Jesus. Why was this so strange?

As a military man, you would expect him to act big and tough and not admit he had a problem. As a Roman you'd expect him to ask for help from other Romans or even Roman gods. As a centurion you would expect him to make demands from a Jew. But the centurion went to Jesus and humbly asked Him to help.

So why's a big macho enforcer requesting help from Jesus? There's only one reason. As a centurion he had the authority of Caesar and the Roman Empire behind him. He gave orders expecting them to be carried out. The centurion believed **JESUS HAD GOD'S AUTHORITY AND POWER.** So, he asked Jesus to give the orders for his servant to be healed, expecting a result. Which is exactly what Jesus did.

Jesus highlighted this centurion's attitude as being the best He had ever come across in Israel. The centurion asked for help believing that God has the power to change the situation. **HOW BIG IS YOUR GOD?** Is your attitude to life one of believing that you must be in control, or of letting God be in control?

>ENGAGE

Where do you take a problem? Inside to bottle it up? Outside to whoever will listen? The first person to share it with is Jesus. Why? The same reason as the centurion went to Jesus. Jesus has the power to do something positive about it and work things out for your benefit. Believing that Jesus has the power to change people and situations will radically change your outlook on life.

BACK TO THE FUTURE

'It will be good for those servants whose master finds them ready, even if he comes in the middle of the night or towards daybreak. But understand this: if the owner of the house had known at what hour the thief was coming, he would not have let his house be broken into. You also must be ready, because the Son of Man will come at an hour when you do not expect him.' **LUKE 12:38–40**

Our attitudes affect our approach to the future. If it's 'me, me, me', we tend to live for 'now, now, now'. If it's 'God, God, God', we take a longer, much different view of the future.

There's an attitude that says 'go for it now while you're young enough to enjoy it'. This encourages us to party today and hope the future works out.

God gives different advice: 'Live for the future.' Today is an opportunity to **ENJOY ETERNITY.** Your life is better for revolving around God and all His future plans. One big event to look forward to is Jesus' return to earth. So it makes sense to live it up with Jesus, not without Him.

Now, if you really see your long-term future as eternity, it affects your whole attitude to life. Instead of living for the buzz of the moment, you'll want to live for God. Instead of booting up each day with a list of 'I wanna dos' you'll ask, 'What does God want me to do?' If we are geared up to thinking that **JESUS COULD RETURN TODAY** – yes, today – it'll alter our whole approach to today. Priorities will change.

>ENGAGE

Only God knows the exact date and time Jesus will return. However, we're encouraged to live our lives as if it is going to be soon. This means you need to be on red alert to make the most of every opportunity you have to serve Him.

PRAY

Lord, thank You for today. Thank You that every new day is a gift and an opportunity from You. Help me to make the most of the day You've given me. Amen.

Few people understood how tough life can be better than the guys in the Old Testament.

Join lion-hearted Daniel, escaping Elijah and a whole host of judges as they rise up to face their challenges with boldness and courage. You'll be encouraged each day to live for God and with God.

978-1-78259-352-2

See how what you believe about God really does affect your life.

Containing short chunks to chew over and real-life stories which take you through themes including 'The character and personality of God' and 'Getting the best out of life' – real living for (and with) God.

978-1-78259-182-5

YP's daily devotional –
dig deeper into God's Word

Never did reading the Bible look so good! Get eye-opening, jaw-dropping Bible readings and notes every day, plus special features and articles in every issue (covers two months).

Available as individual issues or annual subscription. For current prices and to order visit

www.cwr.org.uk/youth

Also available online or from Christian bookshops

Being a Christian sounds great, but what exactly does it involve?

If this is what you have been thinking then this booklet is for you. In just 30 days you can find out how completely mindblowing life with God can be. Each day we explain how you can effectively live for Jesus and start to get to grips with the Bible – His Word to us.

978-1-85345-105-8

Get to know and understand the Bible

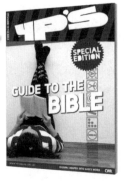

Written to help you know and understand the Bible better, this exciting full-colour guide includes key events, maps, timelines, major characters, explanations of biblical terms and so much more!

978-1-85345-352-6